S.M. BLACKWAY

THINKING CLEARLY

The Ultimate Guide to The Power Of Positive Thinking, Discover and Learn the Effective Strategies to Train Your Mind Towards Positive Thinking to Achieve Success

Descrierea CIP a Bibliotecii Naționale a României
S.M. BLACKWAY
    THINKING CLEARLY. The Ultimate Guide to The Power Of Positive Thinking, Discover and Learn the Effective Strategies to Train Your Mind Towards Positive Thinking to Achieve Success / S.M. Blackway. – Bucharest: Editura My Ebook, 2020
    ISBN 978-606-983-589-0

S.M. BLACKWAY

THINKING CLEARLY

The Ultimate Guide to The Power Of Positive Thinking, Discover and Learn the Effective Strategies to Train Your Mind Towards Positive Thinking to Achieve Success

My Ebook Publishing House
Bucharest, 2020

TABLE OF CONTENTS

FOREWORD

When we turn on the news nowadays there's hardly any good news. Heartwarming stories appear few and far between. It's hard to be positive with so much negative data influencing us each and every day.

To turn positive in our thinking we need to center on things that inspire and uplift us. If we can alter our outlook and do away with the negative thoughts that invade our minds we'll become happier.

If you find it hard to defeat a negative attitude then maybe this book can benefit you by rendering you some positive attitude tips that you can apply in your daily life. Easier said than done, right? Why not give it a attempt.

Here are the ten steps to success thru positive thinking. Many individuals have benefited by utilizing these tips to stop negative thinking and build a more positive attitude.

Positive Thinking Power Play 10 Steps to Success

CHAPTER 1

BE AROUND POSITIVE PEOPLE

Synopsis

Surround yourself with successful and positive people. It's astonishing how the influence of other people can impact and touch on our own personal energy. Positive individuals will energize and urge us to grow in our belief that we can achieve what we set out to do. Head off negative individuals who will ultimately dismantle any progress you make.

The Right People

Positive individuals seem to have a supply of energy that never seems to let them down, and they accomplish the great goals in life that they want and dream about. They can help you remain on track and energize you toward your own goals. A lot of times these successful individuals share the same goals you have and are frequently very generous about passing on their wisdom and their strategies.

So how do you discover these positive, like-minded individuals?

Here are a few tips to help you find them, network with them, and glean useful info and advice:

1. *Smile*. Though it may sound ridiculous, smiling can immediately draw individuals towards you – particularly other positive individuals. Having and showing a good perspective of life's ups and downs makes others want to be around you. It's often hard to stay positive day in and day out, so individuals are often seeking a way to be more optimistic. If you're a friendly welcoming individual, and you show that to the world with your smile, people will see you as an optimistic go-to individual.

You've in all probability heard it takes fewer muscles to smile than to frown, so not only will you be beaming positivism to the world, you'll as well be saving energy.

2. *Convey Positively*. Although we all have rocky days when nothing appears to be going right, the last thing you want do is sound off and whine ceaselessly. No one likes a bellyacher, right?

For instance, if somebody were to ask you, - how are you today? don't crank back that - life stinks or that you're just - alive or something to that impression. Rather, take a minute – and a breath – and then reply with optimism, even if you're having a hard day. After all, positive individuals don't waste their time or energy on bellyachers or negative individuals.

It can be truly difficult to feel positive in the face of life's challenges, and I'm not advising that you suppress your emotions. So either clean out the stuff that's difficult to deal with using a tool like EFT, or choose to center on what is working.

Even if you're not feeling all that positive, by staying optimistic in your outlook you'll still draw in positive individuals to you.

3. *Think Positively.* Thinking positively – even through letdowns – will help you to see the good in every state of affairs and attract the positive individuals who share this vision.

Even if you don't truly subscribe to these positive thoughts at the start, or you discover positive thinking hard, catching yourself in negative self-talk and asking - what do I want alternatively, will help you think positively and produce new patterns of positive thoughts in your brain. Over time positive thinking will get easier and more innate.

We've all got energy inside us and we have the option to use it constructively or destructively. Pay attention to the positive individuals in your life and you'll notice they try to be cheerful and optimistic, even during hard times.

4. *Behave Positively.* It isn't adequate to smile, communicate, and think positively when going after your goal. You must as well take action!

For instance, maybe you thought you could get a promotion in the past, but then sat idly by while somebody else snapped it up. This time your new positive thinking will have metamorphosed you into a positive individual who takes positive action!

Showing your boss and colleagues that you're proactive and positive will set you up for more successes.

5. *Extend.* Lastly, reach out to individuals at your work, in your circle of friends, or even to individuals on the street who seem to live positively. Ask them what it is that helps them remain positive and achieve their objectives.

Looking for positive individuals will give you useful information to help you reach your goals and help you become successful; it will help you establish a network of positive friends and role models.

Being positive and exemplifying positivism draws in other people. After all, like attracts like.

Individuals enjoy being around other people with like attitudes and, by sustaining a positive outlook, you'll surely lead yourself to those successful individuals you seek.

CHAPTER 2

USE POSITIVE AFFIRMATIONS

Synopsis

Think of a positive affirmation and repeat it frequently. Positive affirmations can create amazing results in your thought process. For instance, if you write that you're always depressed then your affirmation may be, "I'm happy I'm in control." Repeat your affirmations many times a day and feel the power of positive thinking. If you can't think of an affirmations then listen to cheerful music or sing happy light hearted lyrics.

Creating Affirmations

All Positive Affirmations are not created equal, as a matter of fact some can even be damaging to changing the habit, paradigm or frame of mind you're trying to change. For instance, you're wanting to quit smoking but you use the affirmation - I will not smoke - by having - not in your affirmation you may actually be reinforcing your smoking habit as the mind tends to omit the - not and only see - I will smoke. Additionally the affirmation is in a future tense by having the word - will in it - so your subconscious interprets that it's not something you're wanting to do right now - it's waiting on the - when statement.

Positive Affirmations ought to be expressed in the present tense.

- I am or - Right now I (present tense) should be used instead of - I will (future tense) as to the subconscious - tomorrow never comes .

Positive Affirmations can be declared as first person or second person.

Research has demonstrated that some individuals respond better to - first person (I) affirmations but other people may react better to - second person (you) affirmations. I'd suggest using both - why not cover all the bases. If you use first person affirmations you can record using a simple microphone attached to your computer and then convert the WAV file to an MP3 file for your MP3 player or - burn to a CD. For - second person you ought to record soul else using the affirmation or use - synthetic voice software.

Positive Affirmations ought to be specific.

Émile Coué, a former pioneer in positive affirmations, used his now famous - Every day, in every way, I'm getting better and better affirmation to reportedly help 1000s of individuals with assorted illnesses. But research in the last few years has demonstrated that the more specific the affirmation the more probable it is to create the desired result. I'm happy and grateful that I'm at my ideal weight of 115 pounds is better than I'm happy and thankful that I'm at my ideal weight. I have no doubt however that even Coué's non-specific affirmation would give you a better total sense of welfare if used consistently.

Positive Affirmations call for repetition to produce results.

When it comes to affirmations repetition is king. In order for the subconscious to act it requires hearing or seeing the affirmation repeatedly. Can you envisage what would happen if the subconscious only needed a couple of repetitions to act? - our lives would be bedlam.

Positive Affirmations are best utilized with emotion.

Just robotically repeating an affirmation won't create the same results as an affirmation which is blended with emotion. Since we're all a bit different it might be helpful to look at some of the different emotions you have and see how you may incorporate them with your affirmation. A few examples for a stop smoking affirmation may be; - ...and whenever I consider a cigarette I tell myself STOP (while pounding your fist into the palm of your other hand - I wouldn't urge this technique if you're in a meeting and your boss is speaking); before repeating your affirmation you could rip a cigarette apart with a lot of anger. You wouldn't want or have to do it each time you heard to our repeated the affirmation - that could get expensive.

Positive Affirmations shouldn't produce any negative side effects.

Be heedful when producing affirmations that you get only the results you want. Using an affirmation like - I'm determined to lose weight and will do whatever it takes to reach my goal of 180 pounds may result in your subconscious saying - okay I can take care of that command - I'll just make you ill - that should help you drop some weight real fast.

Positive Affirmations ought to be realistic.

It's great to employ affirmations to help us engulfed even our biggest challenges but our affirmations just like our goals need to be based in reality (even though truth is often what we think it is). For example if you've always had a - poverty mentality but you use an affirmation that you're richer than Bill Gates I'll predict you'll spend a long time waiting for that affirmation to evidence.

Positive Affirmations ought to be short and sweet.

Affirmations should be long enough to be particular but not so long that they can't be easily restated or remembered.

Positive Affirmations ought to be used consistently.

Utilizing an affirmation once in a while when you think about it will likely not do anything but make you think that affirmations don't work - they have to be used consistently. Your subconscious helps you to accomplish the real desires of your heart and would probably not interpret an occasional affirmation as being a true want. I advocate at least 30 days of the same affirmation, or longer if required.

Positive Affirmations are best utilized along with visualization.

The more ways you impress onto your subconscious your wants the greater the odds of success. Writing or typing your affirmation onto a card that you can carry with you and read at any opportunity will further help your affirmation to manifest. For a few affirmations you can use a photo as a visual affirmation - like an old photo when you were at the weight you now want to be - or possibly your head pasted onto someone else's body. There's likewise some great visualization software available online.

Positive Affirmations need execution to work.

Positive Affirmations without execution is probably not going to manifest. Positive affirmations tho' a very powerful tool are not like your own personal genie - most things you would like to change will call for a little action - like telling yourself to STOP when you're about to do something not in coalition with what you say your goal is. Even the easy action of reading your affirmation card at every chance can produce astonishing results.

Positive Affirmations work best when used with a feel of gratitude.

Saying an affirmation with a sense of gratitude does a few things; firstly it opens your heart up to receive - if you don't have a sense of gratitude you're not in a receptive frame of mind, and 2nd, it's affirming that you already possess the thing you're affirming - which becomes the truth as soon as you accept it per se.

CHAPTER 3

AVOID NEGATIVE THINKING

Synopsis

When you begin using positive affirmations in your daily routine, avoiding negative thinking is just as crucial. Even though this is easier said than done it's a must. It will take forbearance and perseverance but you can take away negative thinking. Your success depends upon blocking the negative thoughts.

Quash The Bad Thoughts

Stopping being negative is like quitting any other bad habit – the more serious the bad habit, the more work it takes to move on the far side of it. Just like it's easier for somebody who smokes two cigarettes per day to quit smoking than it is for somebody who smokes two packs per day, somebody who has an occasional negative thought will have an more comfortable time than somebody who is a chronic bellyacher. But don't fret if you're in the latter class, as long as your commitment is firm, you'll be able to transform your life.

Here are a few tips to help you do away with the negative thoughts in your life:

➤ Set a realistic goal for cutting back your negativity. Saying that you'll never have a negative thought again is unrealistic and will only set yourself up for failure. In most examples, it won't happen overnight so anticipate the entire process to take approximately a month.

➤ Surround yourself with individuals who are positive. You don't have to dump your friends that are negative, but attempt to excuse yourself when conversation topics turn negative and don't take part in - pity parties.

➤ Be cognizant of when you allow negativity to affect you and stop it. Turn it into a positive thing by thinking to yourself - I saw myself saying something negative so I won't do it again next time.

➤ Reward yourself when you avert being negative.

Once again, keep in mind that your goal here is to cut down the amount of negativity in your life and not entirely eliminate it (if you can do the latter, more power to you). Ironically, popular media depicts positive people in a negative way – naïve, weird, out of touch, bothersome, uncool and unpleasant. This is because when individuals are happy and fulfilled they have no need to elude reality by overeating, drinking alcohol, taking drugs (both narcotics and prescription) and bury themselves in television, movies and celebrity gossip to forget about their atrocious lives.

It's perfectly absurd to think this way as in reality positive individuals are the complete opposite – popular, successful and happy. Here's a bonus tip that will help you do away with negativity: turn off the television set and spend some quality time with the individuals you love.

CHAPTER 4

SET GOALS

Synopsis

This is a really crucial step that will help you to be successful in changing your negativity to a more positive mindset. When you set realistic goals it will help you to keep focused.

Achieving a reachable goal will step-up your positive outlook. If you set a goal of making a million dollars in a month which most likely won't happen it will only destroy the efforts you've made to be more positive.

Look Forward

These basic tips are organized in a sequence that will support you from thinking of your goals to actually accomplishing them. These are only suggestions, take what you like and try it out for a while to see what works best for you.

1. Utilize a journal to keep track of your goals journey where you may keep daily or weekly records of your advancement including affirmations, successes, appreciations for your hard work, reinforcements, resistances, obstacles, etc. Use your goals journal to write goals initially and to rescript them over time. Use it to break your goals into steps. Review your progress regularly and jot a few notes.

2. Get yourself into a positive state before writing your goals: It's truly crucial to get yourself into an inspired, positive and relaxed state before writing goals. A few ideas for getting yourself into a positive state include: Meditation, listening to inspiring music, reading something fun or amusing, watching a amusing movie, taking a walk in a naturally beautiful place, brisk exercise, reading or listening to an inspirational story, listening to motivational tapes, brisk exercise or prayer.

3. Begin brainstorming: After getting into a good mental and emotional state, start your brainstorming. Write all potential goals quickly with no editing or criticism. You can review and

prioritise later; right now you want to be as creative and grand in your vision as you are able to be.

4. Areas of your life to consider for goal setting: Here are a number of potential areas of your life to consider when you're formulating your goals list: Career, financial, relationship, family, home, friends, personal development, wellness, appearance, possessions, fun and recreation, travel, spiritual, self-respect and service/community. Some types of goals include: personal development like emotional, mental, physical and spiritual.

5. Goals time frames: Goals fall under varying time periods such: Immediate goals, 30 day goals, 6 month goals, 1 year goals, 5 years, 10 years or longer. Make certain you are able to accomplish what you want in the time frame you set.

6. Here are 4 tips for writing effective goal statements:
Say it like it's already happened: When writing your goal, say it like it's already happened. Put your goals in words that presume that you already have accomplished them. For instance, - I now have a new silver BMW 4 door 2002 sedan.

Utilize motivating language: To get you passionate, committed and motivated, add emotional language to your written goals. Here's an instance - I utterly love and am excited about my beautiful new home in the hills which is much more passionate than - I like my new home in the hills.

Write specifically and in detail: as your subconscious manifests things literally, you want to write particular detailed goals. Use language that's clear in describing exactly what it is you want

Author in positive terms instead of negative ones: Examples of positive statements may be: - I'm now free of the habit of smoking, or - I'm now a smoke free individual. Negative examples may be: - I don't smoke any longer or - I'm not a smoker.

7. Make sure they're really your goals: Check in with yourself to make certain that you're thinking of what you really want. Often we try to please others at our own expense. You won't be successful trying to accomplish the goals your parents, spouse or other friends or relatives want for you.

8. Be congruous in making goals: Consider your most crucial values and beliefs when forging your goals (e.g. honesty,

security, integrity, freedom, responsibility, respect for others, love, leadership, etc.). For example if you value freedom, your goal may be to be self-employed. If security is what you value, you may want to work for the government where layoffs rarely occur.

9. Pick out rational goals: select goals that you can really reach in a reasonable amount of time. An example of a rational goal might be: - I'm 55 years old and I want to sing opera with a local light opera performance group, a choir, or monthly recitals with my voice teacher's students (given of course that you have a good voice). An irrational goal might be: - I'm 55, I've never taken singing lessons, and I want to be a world class opera singer performing key roles with the New York Metropolitan Opera. It's unlikely that anybody starting at the age of 55 could do this, even with an excellent voice and rigorous training.

10. Prioritize your goals: After you've brainstormed, one way to prioritise is to put the highest priority goals at ten out of a possible ten points and the least important at 1 out of 10. Pick 3-7 of the goals with high numbers and center your efforts only on them for the next few months. Try not to pick too many goals

to center on as this will dilute your energy and make it harder to get the results you want.

11. Produce a step-by-step plan: Break each goal down into manageable blocks creating a step-by-step plan to achieve it. For instance, if you want a new car, first decide exactly what color, model, year, and brand you want. Write this down in your goals journal. Then write the particular steps you need to get to your goal like: Apply for a auto loan, look at and test drive different models, write affirmations, visualize yourself driving the car, and so forth.

CHAPTER 5

BE GRATEFUL

Synopsis

When you appreciate all the positive things you have in your life regardless how small it is will help you to successfully abolish negativity. Centering on these good things will make the challenges you face significantly less important and are more easily addressed.

Give Thanks

When something bad happens, instead of embracing it and taking it personally we need to learn to change how we think of it. For instance, if you work in the service industry and you have a rude customer, instead of letting it ruin your day and your mood, try and show some compassion, perhaps something bad has happened to that individual, try and do something nice for them. A smile can be contagious. Instead of taking everyone's bad mood personally make the choice to be in a good mood, smile and circulate the cheer!

With larger life issues that can bring us down, like a ill family member, a divorce, a disagreement with a loved one, cast your worries away. Do what you can to help or correct the situation and then leave it in God's hands. You're only a person, you can't fix everything and shouldn't have to carry all of life's burden's on your heart day in and day out. Do your best to apologise to those you wronged, forgive those who wronged you, ask for help when you require it, and offer help when you are able to.

It's about letting go of all of those things sitting in your heart that are keeping you from having a positive outlook. It's your option, you are able to keep the negative or let it go to make room for the positive.

Some people will never tell you he had a bad day. As a matter of fact some believe there's no such thing as a bad day. This was a hard concept for me to grasp...for me "bad days" had been a steady occurrence. To some every day is a gift. Some are thankful for challenges as they teach him, he is thankful for his job even when it is not pleasant. I marveled at his ability to see each day as a "good day" regardless what happened. When I started to try and adopt this philosophy I detected it worked! Just when I decided in my mind that I was having a "bad day" I'd try and discover something good in it, when I discovered something good I realized that a few bad things don't ruin a whole day unless you let it! Its a option! Every day we're alive is a gift there is so much to be grateful for so why do we center on the things that make us unhappy?

Readapt your thinking...bad days are selections we make!

In the end having a positive outlook is up to you! Its a choice we make day-to-day. You can never control what other people say or do to you but you are able to control your response. By selecting the positive route, as briefly outlined, you'll be happier and healthier than ever before. You'll have a peace within you that will leave people looking at you in awe. I think is a choice that's worth making.

CHAPTER 6

SURROUND YOURSELF WITH POSITIVE

Synopsis

To me, hearing motivational material is empowering and stimulating yet soothing and relaxing at the same time.

Capitalize on the wealth of data on personal accomplishment that's available today and you, as well, will soon be hooked on success.

Drink It In

In the past fifty years approximately, unbelievable progress has been made in the areas of personal achievement and personal development. Individuals have committed their entire lives to the study of success. Their lives' work has been summed up in the books and audio platforms they've released. A lot of these books and platforms sit like concealed gems on shelves of bookstores and in warehouses, awaiting readers to find the life-changing info held inside.

If these books and plans are really that mighty, why don't a lot of individuals read and listen to them? Here are the basic causes:

* They don't believe the data will aid them. This is the most challenging obstruction for success writers to defeat. It requires belief, or faith, for a person to begin reading a book, begin listening to an audio course of study, or begin a program like this one. Ironically, a lot of these plans contain info that will help establish the faith needed; all the same, those without at least a little trust, or a willingness to retain an open mind, will never take that step.

* Self-help content has gotten a foul "rap". In a few cases, this is well merited. There are a few writers, particularly on the matter of making income, that are, well... let's simply say less than certified to be giving advice. If you're purchasing a book on how to make a million bucks, is the writer a millionaire? Did he get to be a millionaire by marketing his "how to be a millionaire" books? Study about the writer(s) before you purchase a book or audio plan. Study reviews and see what other people have said.

* They didn't feel they got anything out of former programs they've attempted. At the very least, their minds were submitted to hours of positive mental disciplining. It's actually really hard to pick up a book or listen to an audio plan and not acquire at least one beneficial idea or even life-changing concept. Seek that one idea and most of the time you'll discover many.

Now here are scarcely a few of the benefits of reading and listening to positive, motivational, and educational content.

* Never feel like you're wasting time again. How much time do you expend a week driving in your car, sitting on public transportation, exercising, or doing any other action in which you're, or may be, listening to material of your choice? How much time do you expend waiting; in lines, for engagements, or for other people? This may be turned into some of your most useful time spent.

* It's motivational. We're already cognizant of the might of motivation. Read or listen to the words of additional optimists that inspire you and give you mental might to do nearly anything you set your mind to.

* It's educational. Training shouldn't stop after highschool or college. To develop as an person we should spend

our lives fertilizing our brains with valuable info. Just like a lot of careers that necessitate ongoing training via seminars and conferences, you should take ongoing education for your own personal accomplishment. Your success in living depends on it.

* We all require suitable mental training. From the time we were added into this earth till the present day, our minds have been programmed with negativity and confining beliefs. Some of this comes from our rearing, friends, colleagues, the news we read and the commercials we watch. By centering on positive material, we can virtually recondition our minds and substitute the negative, constraining beliefs we have about success with positive, endowing ones.

Here is a process for capturing the most out of non-fictional, self-help content.

1. *Study for comprehending.* Personal development plans are jammed with data and tips that work best when they're retained in your conscious memory. Study or listen to the book or tape more than one time. Each time you do, your retentiveness of the info increases. Don't absorb too much data at a time. The average mind begins to drift and meander

someplace between twenty and thirty minutes. When this occurs, call for a break.

2. *Assess*. You surely don't have to trust everything you read or hear. Assess what the writer has to say with an clear mind. Does it add up to you? If you followed the belief, would it better your life? If so, why not give it a effort? Don't be put off by the writer even if you don't agree with most of what is stated. Take what you are able to from the plan and leave the remainder.

3. *Implement*. It's said that knowledge without application isn't might; it's only likely might. Utilize and implement what you learn to your daily life. Only then will the info be of real worth to you.

4. *Recap*. Return to your books, tapes, notes, and plans often and consider the times you've utilized the data. When you come across the benefits, it will produce a passion for learning keener than you've ever had earlier.

5. *Contribution*. Make these books, tapes, and plans easily available to those you care about. Most individuals won't spend just a couple of dollars purchasing their own book or tape, but they might just read or listen to it if it's there.

CHAPTER 7

GET ORGANIZED

Synopsis

Commit yourself to a positive environment. If your environment is littered and disorganized spend the time to get organized it will go a long way in helping you to alter your thinking. Who can be positive sitting in the midst of a mess? An organized environment is elating and inspiring, a great place to establish a positive attitude.

Get Moving

So you need to get organized. Well, so do we all. But now that you've set the organizing goal, how do you successfully carry off the ins and outs of achieving it? Here are some tips to do just that.

1. Begin with the correct job

This is crucial. Separate your organizing effort into sensible and traceable tasks, prioritize and begin with a job which you believe will give you the most bang for the sweat you put into organizing it and getting it completed. folders are bang-up tools This could be a littler job, which you know will be completes fast enough, giving you the much required motivation booster to move on to the next greater projects that you've been dreading.

Or instead, it could be a larger job which you know was crying for your attention for a while now, and getting it off your plate will take the most burden off your mind.

Take a moment if you need to determine this.

That time is advantageously spent, compared to the likely hours you may expend on a certain task, only to leave it unfinished in the midst.

2. Don't get side-tracked with micro- sub-tasks

This is likely the common reason why trying to get organized bombs for a lot of individuals.

You begin organizing something, like say your photograph albums, and then begin to look at those photos and slip back into memories.

Before you recognize, a few hours have passed, and you might have even had a blast, but - those albums haven't moved.

A different example would be attempting to organize a bunch of papers, only to digress when you get to those tax papers, and begin calculating your tax refund.

Be methodical and operative about it; if essential, set yourself a sensible time limit to finish each job, and make adhering to it a priority.

Tell yourself once you're set organizing, you'll relax and spend an hour browsing those albums, perhaps sipping a well merited drink.

3. Produce a temporary staging area

While clearing up your clutter, at times you may bump into items for which you haven't made a space for, and are not sure where to place them. You've 2 alternatives to deal with them:

You can either spend a little time to think through where they go, and set them there. You can group like things together, and assign a basic place holder for them, founded on where you require them the most.

Instead, if you feel that working out what to do with them is taking a bit much time, or distracting you from your total organization attempt, you can set them in a "temporary staging area", like a cardboard carton, with a mental note (or a sticky note) to return to it once the rest of it's done.

A caution, though - if you begin tossing everything you have a question about into this temporary place, before long it will become one more muddle which you'll finally have to deal with. And that kills its purpose.

4. Don't multi-task

Don't be lured to try and get everything done right away. While this might seem more effective, in the long haul it doesn't turn out to be, as chances are it might lead to jumping to and fro between tasks, and you may wind up not finishing anything.

Instead, assign a task or a portion of the task to somebody else, if that's workable.

5. Do not be a perfectionist

Finally but not the least, don't be a perfectionist in attempting to fit everything in exactly specified places. Be flexible. Recognize that everything can't be perfect, and as long as you know where your things are, and are able to get to your items with no effort, you're organized, even if it looks like clutter to the next individual.

Now that we have got the jumble out of the way and know how to get organized, make sure you stay organized, and take the daily actions to pursue to keep it that way.

CHAPTER 8

STAY FOCUSED

Synopsis

Focus on positive things in your daily life. Don't center on the things you don't want or the mistakes that happen. If you shift your thoughts to the situation at hand, then you leave no room for the anxious thoughts to command your thinking.

Get It Together

Hold an impression of what you want to accomplish at all times, this pulls it to be manifested inside your life. View yourself there and try to feel how you would if you were there already. The only thing that's keeping you from being there is you and entirely you, so let yourself be there in any way imaginable. We're all able of accomplishing our goals; it's just a matter of time. By visualizing or acting as if you already accomplished your goals, you'll discover new focus on why you're working towards your goals.

If you're like me and working entirely alone to achieve these goals you've set for yourself, then I advise breaking that work up into littler pieces. It's best and easier to work as though you're making a jigsaw puzzle, rather than making a 20 foot wall painting. This will help keep you motivated and centered due to the fact that you're unceasingly achieving small pieces of the goals.

Don't listen to the nay-sayers, if somebody thinks you're a bit nuts, or don't have trust in what you can achieve, then forget about them.

These individuals are just a bit upset that they don't have the drive, as you do, to aim for the stars. Don't entirely blame them either; it's just that society has a way of disciplining individuals into persisting in their safe and cozy comfort zones. If you let them affect you, your centering will disperse, and we don't want that.

Remain out of your comfort zone; being successful is all about accepting risks and doing what is generally not done in our society – taking the path lower traveled. If you persist in your comfort zone, you'll be at ease and that may lead you to blanking out your goals – drifting in limbo while you look for something to happen is never beneficial. Avoid your comfort zone, if you're sort of uncomfortable it might mean that you're climbing higher into new and unchartered soil you've never been in, and that's exactly where you want to be.

Check everything you've achieved at the end of the week to supercharge yourself, and then see what are your approaching tasks for the next week. This exercise keeps you centered by furnishing you with hard facts about where you've been and where you're going next. Always put down everything that you have been doing and anything you wish to do. Use a planner, a calendar, excel, word, or whatsoever you want to use to put down everything, and go over it once or twice a week – but merely do it.

Among the things that's always helped me with my goals is discussing them. I'll discuss where I am, troubles I need to fix, fresh goals I have brought to my list, or how much work I have left to achieve any of them. By talking about your goals to trusted friends and even family members, you make support for your thoughts, and hey who knows, they might even help you see something you haven't. It's always good to let it out, don't keep it in as though it was a secret – silence isn't the way, you need to discuss it.

Occasionally it's helpful to walk off from a particular project or goal your working towards for a few days to let it brew in your mind. You may discover that once you rejoin it, you might have a fresh perspective angle towards it that you might not have had before. This is where your mind subconsciously solves problems it couldn't before, due to the fact that you never gave yourself the time to sop it in. It's the same way as though you planted a seed, if you endlessly stare at it for many days it may not seem as it's growing, but if you walk off for a few days and come back to it, you'll observe new things about it. This will fuel you, pulling in a new found focus in accomplishing your goals.

Among the most crucial things to keep in mind, is that when you're closest to resigning is when you're in fact closest to accomplishing your goals. If you feel like you urgently need to quit on your goals, don't. I've been in a lot of situations where I can't seem to continue on, but that's only a mental roadblock, a conditioned thing you have inside you that's trying to undermine you from accomplishing your goals. We're all prone to this pressure and most circum to it. Don't follow the masses, you're different, if you continue, you'll probably succeed. Just keep at it, and you'll soon savor the real fruits of your labor.

Most individuals keep work and life on separate sides of the spectrum, when in fact you need to mix them together in a appropriate balance. Working isn't negative, and forever try to keep this mentality. It's among the things that gives us worth. By making your work part of your daily life, your goals will be accomplished at an overall smoother and better rate and you'll sustain a healthy focus.

Though you must forever remember to keep a balance, don't be swallowed by either or, you won't be useful to anybody if you burn out.

Don't ever let yourself burn out, and if you do, take a holiday or something. I'm very ambitious towards all my goals, but I as well respect - time out sessions once in a while. If you get nauseated just by looking at something you're suppose to be working at, then just leave it for a while and work at something else or try to unwind. If you make time to unwind then you'll refresh yourself. Each one of us has our certain cap of leeway towards any given thing before we need to recharge again. Know and respect your tolerance cap. Keep it balanced and even if you - have to do something – blow it off. By presenting yourself time to recharge and unwind, you're in turn replenishing your focus meter so that you can continue without handicapping your productivity.

CHAPTER 9

USE TIME WISELY

Synopsis

Avoid spending time on activities that don't agree with what you want in life. The crucial thing is to consistently work towards the activities that will make your life what you want and this in turn will help you have a positive attitude.

Time Is Precious

There are 24 hours in a day. At a first glimpse it seems a great deal, but in our practical every day experience we often feel that there's never enough time to do all the things that we want to do. How can we apply our time in such a way that we can get the most out of those 24 hours?

A successful businessman once stated, "If you want to be successful in life you have to forfeit either sleep or television or both." There's much soundness in these words. To use time wisely the beginning thing we can do is to become conscious of where we are not utilizing time wisely - put differently: where we feel we're wasting time. TV has brought a lot of good things, but it's also true that it can take over much of our precious time unnecessarily. We can apply the time we save by watching less TV by doing something constructive in our own lives or by doing something good for humankind.

It goes without saying that sleep is utterly necessary and essential. But some of the times we tend to indulge ourselves in acquiring more sleep than we really need - particularly on the weekend. So if we really prefer to write that novel, master that difficult piece on the piano or work out that fabulous business plan, we might have to become more economical in our sleeping conduct.

Eight hours of sleep are suggested for sound health. Yet through the practice of meditation we can step by step reduce the amount of sleep we require. From eight hours it can become seven hours, six hours or even five or four hours, contingent on our individual capacity. For meditation provides us inner peace, which can replace an amount of outer sleep. It's said that a moment of real inner peace which one can experience in deep meditation can substitute several hours of sleep.

A different thing which might help us in using time more effectively is to alter activity once in a while. By altering activity we give ourselves a break. For our mind everything gets boring and tedious after a while, so if we venture into a fresh activity the mind gets new exuberance and energy. That new joy and energy will as well help us to work much more concentrated and effectively. Then when we get enough of that task we can once again return to the former task and we'll again get new joy and enthusiasm. "Rest is change of activity," some spiritual teachers say. If we know how to utilize this little phrase of wisdom in our every day lives, we'll be taking a big step forwards towards the fulfillment of our ambitions.

CHAPTER 10

GET THE CORRECT ATTITUDE

Synopsis

If you're not happy with your life then it's up to you to alter it.

By developing the right attitude you are able to achieve anything you set your sights on.

Look At It The Right Way

Attitude isn't quite everything when it concerns being successful, but attitude plays a part in almost every phase of your life. A pitiful attitude gets more individuals fired than any other single factor, and a good attitude gets individuals jobs and helps them keep those jobs more than any other factor.

Your attitude bears on many individuals, from your family to the stranger you smile at on the street corner. Your attitude is especially important when you face apparently hopeless situations. Losing a job, mate, or friend because of a lousy attitude is unfortunate - particularly because a bad attitude can be doctored

You can find at least 2 ways to view virtually everything. A pessimist seeks difficulty in the opportunity, whereas an optimist seeks opportunity in the difficulty. A poet of long since put the difference between optimism and pessimism this way: "Two men looked out from prison bars - one saw mud, the other saw stars."

Regrettably, many individuals look only at the trouble and not at the opportunity that lies inside the problem. Many employees complain about the difficultness of their jobs, for instance, not realizing that if the job were easy, the employer would hire somebody with less ability at a lower wage. A little coin can hide even the sun if you hold the coin close enough to your eye. So when you get too close to your troubles to think objectively about them, try to keep in mind how your vision can be blocked, take a step back, and view the situation from a fresh angle. Look up rather than down.

Pessimism muddies up the water of opportunity. Anytime a fresh innovation appears promising to make life easier, somebody always complains that it will take the jobs of individuals. When Eli Whitney invented the cotton gin, objectors said that it would put thousands of individuals out of work. Rather, the invention made the production of cloth much cheaper, and millions of individuals could afford more clothing, which created infinite jobs. When the computer was devised, folks believed that individuals would lose their jobs. Some individuals have had to retrain themselves to stay sellable, but almost everybody agrees that computers have created - not deleted - jobs and have improved our capabilities boundlessly.

You can't do anything to alter the fact that a problem exists, but you can do a good deal to find the opportunity within that problem.

You're guaranteed a better tomorrow by doing your best today and formulating a plan of action for the tomorrows that lie ahead. Just remember to sustain a positive mental attitude so that, as you plan for tomorrow, you're doing so with the sense of anticipation that produces substantially better results.

Faultfinders still believe that someone pushed Humpty Dumpty, and they'd vote against starting a Pessimist's Club as they don't believe that such a club can work.

Almost half of American workers fall into the cynic class. They distrust just about everything - government, big business, the products they purchase, their employer, supervisors, and coworkers. An additional portion of workers is classed as wary, with strong cynical leanings.

How many friends and how much peace do cynics have? How well do they get along with their spouses, children, and neighbors? Not many, not much, and not very well.

On the sunnier side of life are the idealists - persons who have the tendency to see the best solution in any position. Sow those optimistic seeds, and you raise the optimist shrouded inside you.

Much cynicism is induced by unrealistic expectations - expecting great things to happen to you without any effort on your part. Having high anticipations for yourself is a crucial part of success, but you must as well develop a solid goals program to make those anticipations a reality. Individuals too often view the world through rosy glasses, and when their unrealistic expectations come short, they become cynical and put on woes-colored glasses.

Have you ever been stuck in a traffic jam at the worst possible time? Did you stamp your foot, pound the wheel, shake your fist, and rest on the horn? If so, did you discover that the louder you blew your horn and the fouler you got when you shook your fist, the more quickly the traffic ahead of you opened up and let you go through?

If you follow that foot-stomping, horn-blowing act often enough, you raise your blood pressure, step-up your chances of having a heart attack or getting ulcers, and generally ruin your disposition and shorten your life.

Consider that traffic jam, smile, and say, "crikey! I'll bet it's going to take at least half-hour to get through this mess! In half-hour, if I listen to informational tapes, add to my vocabulary, find new leadership principles, or step-up my knowledge!" Or if you have somebody in the car with you, a traffic jam is a chance for an uninterrupted visit. Use the time to complete a grocery list or plan a surprise for your partners next birthday. Your choices may not be bountiful, but using your time to do meaningful things sure beats "stewing without doing."

You do have an alternative - either you can gain or achieve something while you wait, or you can get distressed and bring on strokes, heart attacks, and hypertension. "People jams" in the office, home, neighborhood, school, playground, and ballpark can be addressed in a similar manner. Though you might not be able to pop in a tape or read a book when others schedules don't conform to yours, you can still unwind and people-watch or use the extra time to work at ideas. You'll be healthier and happier at the end of your day if you take that approach.

Wrapping Up

Sustain your focus and you are able to become a positive individual. Now is the time to adopt these powerful mind success techniques and you'll live a happier, more gratifying life now and into the future.

Hopefully this book has given you the tools begin on the path to becoming more positive.

Printed by Libri Plureos GmbH in Hamburg, Germany